# Natural preneurs

# Natural preneurs

### Building Your *Successful* and Scalable Integrative Medical Practice

## DR. JAQUEL PATTERSON, ND, MBA

## NATURALPRENEURS

*I dedicate this to my father, who has always pushed me to strive in all ways in my life, whatever and wherever I am, and to my mother, who is absolutely the strongest woman I know. They both inspire and fuel me every day.*

# Table of Contents

# Introduction

The intention behind this book is to share my medical and business acumen and strengths to support other integrative medicine practitioners in having successful and thriving medical practices, while also maintaining their sanity, schedule, and ability to apply self-care practices. It is often a tricky balance, but my intention is to provide guidance so that you may grow, be successful, and avoid making some of the mistakes I've personally made along the way or spending needless hours working inefficiently.

Having grown up in a large, close-knit family, I've found that connections and support are vital to who I've become as a person. In my adolescence, my mother became sick with lupus. I remember feeling at the time that her case was not treated holistically and her medical care was disregarded. I vowed that I would never be that kind of doctor, someone who didn't look at a patient as a full person and didn't utilize a comprehensive approach. Upon entering Cornell University as a plant science major, I was on a medical track program to go directly to medical school without the MCAT; however, the conventional medical track didn't resonate with me, as I had a passion for integrative medicine and I didn't understand how that could fit into a hospital-based model. I learned more about naturopathic medicine after graduating, and I knew it was a perfect fit for my interest, so I enrolled at the University of Bridgeport College of Naturopathic Medicine after working a few years within the business realm.

Along the way, I became very strong in my business acumen while practicing part-time and scaling the corporate ladder as a healthcare executive. My positions over a span of ten years included chief operating officer and vice president with a focus on operations and quality improvement; I also served as a compliance officer. I managed multi-million-dollar budgets and at some points in my career had over eighty staff under my purview. My passion and heart, though, have always been in naturopathic medicine; it is core to who I am.

My work in healthcare leadership enabled me to help influence the current models of care, particularly for the patient-centered medical home. In addition to serving as the only naturopathic doctor on the Provider Advisory Council for the Person-Centered Medical Home for the state, I provided leadership as the chair for the Integrative Medicine Taskforce for the state Department of Mental Health and Substance Use, and also served in the quality improvement committee for the State Innovation Model. In the naturopathic profession, I serve as the current president for the American Association of Naturopathic Medicine and as the board director for the Connecticut Association of Naturopathic Medicine. I'm a highly sought-after speaker nationally and internationally, I give presentations and train doctors at large and renowned conferences, and I've appeared on television, podcasts, and radio.

I currently run an integrative medical practice in Fairfield, Connecticut, and serve as a medical advisor for Zycal Bioceuticals Healthcare. My medical practice incorporates my vision of how healthcare should be delivered through collaboration, where the core is based on preventive medicine, nutrition, and lifestyle; our goal is for our patients to thrive in their health—which is not purely about the absence of illness. Our team continues to grow and currently consists of four naturopathic physicians, a nutritionist, a physical therapist, an internal medicine consultant, a mental health therapist, and practitioners of craniosacral therapy and reiki therapy. We each have specific niches, and due to our specialty areas, a good proportion of our patients are from out of state; we additionally provide telemedicine services for our patients. Doctors become doctors to serve those in need, and I think at times we as doctors become lost along the way due to the current healthcare infrastructure and its limitations. My journey along this way—running a medical practice, offering products and services, having a dispensary, and managing audits and compliance requirements—is all reviewed in this book to help deter some common pitfalls in running your integrative medical practice. Additionally, this book is about thriving not only in your business, but also personally, and it is important that you are serving yourself and your patients in all the work you may do. Because if not, what is the point of it all?

# Chapter 1

# Types of Practitioners in Integrative Medicine

Integrative medicine became popular in the United States as early as the 1800s. While some parts were adopted into conventional medicine, such as herbs which later became translated into pharmaceutical products, other practices never became mainstream. Because of this, there is a lack of clarity regarding professional designations and training for integrative medicine, especially with the continued growth in this field. As a licensed naturopathic physician, it is important to understand skill level, training, and application as it pertains to being an integrative medicine practitioner.

To start off, here are some definitions plus some basic information regarding practitioner types and education for integrative medicine:

**Naturopathic doctors/physicians** (NDs) have completed a four-year graduate level naturopathic medical program and are educated in all of the basic medical sciences, but also have studied holistic and non-toxic approaches to disease prevention and wellness. Naturopathic doctors complete over 1,500 basic science and clinical hours and over 2,000 hours in both allopathic therapeutics and preceptorships. NDs that are licensed need to pass two board licensing exams and complete jurisprudence in the state they practice in. Currently, there are twenty-two states licensed for naturopathic medicine; the most updated list and information regarding the profession can be found on www.naturopathic.org.

**Chinese medicine** (TCM) or **acupuncture practitioners** have completed a master's degree from an accredited program. In order to be become a licensed acupuncturist, you must complete an exam and certification.

A **functional medicine practitioner** is a broader term. There are multiple applications of being a functional medicine practitioner; most healthcare practitioners can participate in certification programs both online and in-person to become credentialed by a formal association. A healthcare practitioner must have completed a specific educational level and/or have a healthcare license. Most common practitioners with a functional medicine certification include MDs, DOs, NDs, nurse practitioners, DCs, and nutritionists. Naturopathic doctors' core training and curriculum includes functional medicine amongst many other modalities; therefore, they may not seek a functional medicine certification type since it largely exists within the core of their academic and clinical training.

**Chiropractic doctors** have completed a four-year graduate level program from an accredited council on chiropractic education. The licensing process in all states requires completion of a doctor of chiropractic degree program and passing of the national board certification, including a patient encounter.

**Nutritionists** may vary in their level of training and their competence. There are various certification types for nutrition, including a certified nutrition specialist and a certified clinical nutritionist, amongst others. **Dieticians**, in contrast, complete a four-year study with over nine hundred supervised clinical hours, and are primarily based in hospital settings.

*Chapter 2*

# Setting the Right Intention: Mindset

## INTENTION SETTING AND AFFIRMATIONS

Setting intentions and having a determined mindset is, in my experience, the initial starting point in beginning a successful integrative practice, and in building a successful business in general. It's your intention that builds your brand and ultimately is the guiding force behind the culture of your business. It influences your setup process, the mission of the organization, the staff you hire, and, ultimately, where you see your future growth and development. Is your mindset for your business positively directed and proactive, or is it largely reactive and fear-based? If it's the latter, it is much harder to navigate the rollercoaster of having a business. Personally, I have a very different view of failure; I do not see things as failures, but rather as lessons and opportunities to get to where I want faster. I'm unphased by it; I'm tenacious and, though I may not have the answers to everything, I find a way to get those answers and I know when to ask. If this is not your starting base, it is important to make that shift before embarking on such a large journey. If you do not have that type of mindset when going into running a business, it will be difficult for you to weather the storms when they appear. Mindset is key in a business and in life—so if you don't have it, get it quickly by the end of this book!

## SELF-CARE

Self-care has been a central core factor in my life while simultaneously being an area which I struggle with. In school, we learn "doctor, heal thyself"; are you always seeking to embody this in your work? Do you want to have a successful seven-figure business, but work sixteen hours a day for decades? How do you define self-care?

It is equally important to write out not only your business goals, but also your personal goals and your ideal dream of how you want your practice to run. You need to invest time in considering what both your personal and business goals are, and how they will intersect and simultaneously be fulfilled as you grow your practice. For some, it may mean seeing four patients a day, or working only two days a week, and for others, it means having more vacation time. Decide on that, and when building your vision, make this part of fulfilling that dream. This is what keeps you focused on the end goal you have in mind, since it is coupled with your ultimate personal and business benefit. Isn't that why we are going into being an entrepreneur and integrative medicine practitioner? We try to teach others how to incorporate self-care to improve their health passionately and to serve and disrupt the healthcare system as we currently see it. You need to fill your well in order to help others fill theirs, so please make sure that at least once a week, your personal goal is reviewed along with your professional goal. I personally do this by looking at my calendar over the course of several months and intentionally blocking a few days for self-care; for me, it is about time with nature, spas, massages, and energy healing. When you block your schedule to do this, it provides a sense of freedom and reward for the many hours you commit to your business.

## STRATEGIC THINKING

So, now that we've reviewed mindset and affirmations, the next step is to strategically consider what type of business you are looking to create. Is it a practice with a general fee for service, is it concierge- or telemedicine-based, do you want staff, do you want to grow an empire like I dream of, or do you want to be able to work and see patients on your computer while you travel abroad or stay in the recesses of your home? Part of the process of strategic thinking is to initially think big. I think big by jotting down my big ideas on a notepad; from there, assess, assess, assess, and think long-term. Consider if this strategy allows you to meet your business, financial, and personal goals. It is important to build time to reflect; sadly, in our society, being able to make time for reflection is difficult. We are told to act now. I am an act-now personality, but when you are making a big strategic decision, it is important to build in reflection time in a quiet place every week to let your thoughts become clearer. You can do this by blocking your schedule for one hour a week to commit a dedicated amount of time toward your strategic goals.

## MISSION AND VISION STATEMENT

As you build your business, it is important to develop a mission and vision statement from the beginning. This same principle applies if you are looking to acquire a practice; does the mission and vision statement resonate with you? If it does not, this is not a practice to purchase; it needs to resonate with you in some way or you will have more difficulty building a profitable business. A solid mission statement will inspire your business in the present and the future. Generally, a mission statement should be very brief, no longer than a paragraph, and demonstrate the purpose of the company. It should succinctly describe what your business offers, why, the competencies, and the purpose. You should also create a value statement, which shows how the company values the clients they serve and the community at large. Value statements should reflect core priorities, e.g. quality, integrity, customer service, etc. It helps to provide greater definition to the mission statement by outlining clear goals and priorities of focus for your practice. The mission and vision statement also help to direct you when your business scales to ensure you are meeting the philosophy of what you intended to create. Mission and vision statements can also adjust and grow, just like you do as a person. You should consider your business a living, breathing entity that will naturally have its milestones of growth as well as obstacles to cure. Your mission and vision statement should be reviewed every three years to ensure they reflect the current operations of your business.

## CREATING YOUR CULTURE

In my eyes, culture is absolutely everything! The culture you convey should be built upon the vision of how you feel healthcare should be provided, without any limitations or preconceived notions. What culture are your patients coming into, and how is it reflected throughout all aspects of your business? For example, what is the feeling that is created when a patient walks in the door? Does it match with the mission and vision statement goals, or does it feel like what they are used to experiencing in healthcare?

I wanted to provide an environment where the culture was palpable, where a patient can walk away saying "that feels different" or "why aren't my other experiences in healthcare like this?" I was determined to create a culture where patients can come as they are and feel safe and in a trusting environment, where you are greeted and valued in all aspects of care. That is my vision for healthcare, and is why I've chosen to write this book, because I fundamentally believe the healthcare experience should be radically different than the way it currently is. Integrative medicine should be at the core of care and everything should stem from there, and the patients and doctors are part of that journey. This is my vision of my culture and is what drives my decisions as my business grows, and also influences who I choose to have work with me, including contractors, who I partner with, and who I network with. Your culture may be about efficiency, or may incorporate your own personal style and authenticity. Deliberate on this and think clearly before opening your business; or, if you've already started, most certainly think about it now, as well as when you're looking to hire staff. These are all critical points to continued success as your business grows, because they will permeate many aspects of your business, including which patients will naturally be attracted to you, what staff you hire and retain, and what the experience being delivered to those you serve is like.

## POWER HOUR AND PLANNING

I am the ultimate planner. I love plans upon plans, and envisioning what those future plans are—part of my Myers Briggs INTJ-ishness. If you aren't a planner, you must learn to become one quickly. It doesn't mean you need to be an expert, but you should at least begin in small ways. For me, it starts big picture: what are my year-long goals, what are my monthly goals, what are my weekly goals, and what are my daily goals. Starting with your yearly goal and working backward helps make this process much easier in my opinion, whereas for others, it may be easiest starting with today and building from there. It's important to begin with a planner to help keep track of this, but it is more important that you put your plans and that planner of yours into practice. It's nice to draft up a vision board or a plan for the year, month, and week, but if you don't pick it up for another year or look at it, you are wasting your time. I recommend planning a power hour every day; ideally in the morning, but if this doesn't work, perhaps during a different time of day. Create a power hour checklist to review in that hour, e.g. where you are with weekly goals, your financial numbers, or planning a to-do list for the day. Do not use this time to complete charting, respond to emails, review labs, etc. This time should be all about your business and planning. An hour is ideal, but oftentimes even fifteen to thirty minutes a day will make a significant impact on your business. I often have a strong fifteen-minute timeframe, and accomplish so much from that short period of time. That time may build up to two or three hours per week and eight to twelve hours in a month; it will substantially impact your business in a positive way.

# Chapter 3

# Setting Up Your Business

## NAMING YOUR BUSINESS

As you decide on the formation of your business, you can start to narrow down the name of the business you are creating. Naming your business can feel daunting or like a barrier to moving forward. For me, it has always been a stumbling block, and one that requires ample brainstorming, reflection, and decision-making. There are many tips and factors that can help aid in deciding on the name. Here are some key considerations:

- Do not be too specific: You do not want the name to be so specific that it makes it hard for your business to grow in the future. For example, I could easily call my office. Fairfield Lyme Disease Center, since over half of the patients we serve have Lyme disease and other tick-borne infections. However, my practice also serves many patients that do not have Lyme disease, and close to 40 percent are not from Connecticut at all, let alone from Fairfield, Connecticut. This would make my practice too narrowly focused, as it's limiting and wouldn't fully match the patients we serve.

- Use something memorable: Select a name that is memorable. But be mindful of names that are too tricky to spell or difficult for someone to remember.

- Set up domain names and social media handles: If you have narrowed things down to a handful of names, be sure to see if the URL is available. Ideally, you would have a .com URL versus other options. In addition, check to see if you're able to get social media names that match the domain name you've selected and the name of the business. Purchasing a domain is fairly cheap; it's generally cheaper than $20 annually, unless it needs to be purchased from an existing person that has the website name. Often, if you have a name that resonates, it may make sense to obtain the domain name and save it for a later time. Please do remember to renew if you plan to potentially use that domain in the future, otherwise, it will be turned over and someone else may claim your previously held domain name and charge you thousands of dollars to purchase it back. I had this very experience myself, and had to change a domain name since my URL expired/lapsed and I forgot to renew the domain name, even though I had wanted to continue use of it in the future.

- Complete a search: Ensure that the name is not already trademarked; you can visit uspto.gov to confirm. It is not necessary to initially trademark your name unless you feel one hundred percent confident in using that name for a long period of time. Most individuals start with searching for their potential business name in the state they intend to work in, typically with the Secretary of State, to see if it is available. I would HIGHLY recommend that you obtain the domain name prior to submitting an application to register the business name. Once the business name is registered, it is posted, and others can find the name and purchase the domain, causing you to need to buy it from them.

- Consider if it represents your brand: Does the name represent the brand and the mission you are trying to convey? Ideally, the message is easily conveyed by the name. For some, it may make sense based on what the individuals in the population you serve are used to. For example, our business is named Fairfield Family Health, the reason being that we are located in Fairfield, but reside in Fairfield County, which is a larger catchment area. The name, Fairfield Family Health, can translate to towns within Fairfield County. Also, the prior owner of the business used the words "Family Health" so the name was consistent with what patients were accustomed to, and also better for things like search engine optimization.

- Brainstorm: Jot down numerous names. I use the journal notepad in my cellphone and jot down names as I think of them. Sometimes the names come up in the most random of moments: in the shower, upon waking, when having a conversation with friends, etc. Also, make sure you are happy with the name and feel confident saying it out loud. When thinking of names, you may want to put a mix of names together and Google them. There are also some companies that help generate business names—for example, Wordlab Business Name Generator, Business Name Generator, Name Mesh, and Shopify Business Name Generator—to assist with this process.

## FORMATION OF VARIOUS BUSINESS TYPES

There are many different types of business formation. Now that you have more clarity on your mission, vision, and culture, it will inform what business type you are looking to develop. The business types we will discuss include sole proprietor, LLC, LLP, PLLC, corporation, and S corporation. Each have pros and cons that you need to carefully review before making a decision on your business.

**Sole proprietor:** In a sole proprietor, you are the complete and exclusive owner of the business. There is also no separation legally in its existence from the owner. Sole proprietors are easy to set up and establish; however, they are also the greatest risk legally, since it is not a legal entity and the owner is responsible for all debts.

**LLC:** A limited liability corporation (LLC) is considered a hybrid entity. The owners are not responsible for the debts and liabilities of the organization. You are able to hire employees as an LLC, but will need to obtain an EIN and file employment taxes.

**LLP:** A limited liability partner (LLP) is a partnership where the partners have some limited liabilities. A partner may not be eligible for another partner's practices or misconduct.

**PLLC:** A professional limited liability company (PLLC) operates much like an LLC, except it is only available for licensed professionals, e.g. doctors, lawyers, accountants, etc. The services offered are specific to their profession only.

**Corporation:** A corporation is typically a group of people, but can be an individual, that acts as a single entity. It is separate from the owners and it can have contracts and hire employees. A corporation may have shareholders as well; most states only require one person to become a corporation.

**S corporation:** An S corporation is a specific tax election; it is not a business structure, and is commonly misperceived as its own entity type. They can have shareholders, but are limited to no more than one hundred, unlike LLCs and corporations. Both a corporation and an LLC are eligible for S corporation status. There is a specific amount of time, i.e. seventy-five days, allowed once formation is complete to file for S corporation status; for this reason, it is important to ensure the timely completion of any necessary information. S corporations have officers and directors, with a Board of Directors overseeing the affairs of the company; you can, however, have one single officer and director.

## BUSINESS LICENSE AND EMPLOYER IDENTIFICATION NUMBER (EIN)

As soon as you complete the formation of your business, you need to immediately submit for a business license. New business owners sometimes lose initial sight of this, but it is a mandatory requirement for your business. In addition to a business license, you may need a sales and use tax permit, particularly if you are selling products like supplements. Business licenses verify your business and legally protect you, and are needed for taxes. There are various types of business licenses. The most commonly used ones in private practice are business licenses, a sales tax license, a health department permit, a building permit, a zoning permit, fire and police department permits (if you own the property) and withholding tax registration. You also need to get federal and state employer identification numbers (EINs) to identify your business so they can tax accordingly. EINs are not required for every business, but are mandatory for corporations or partnerships. For sole proprietors or LLCs, you may also have a personal tax identification number (TIN) rather than using a social security number for tax purposes. Most LLCs will need an EIN, especially if they have employees or if the filing of excise tax forms is needed. An EIN can be applied for on irs.gov by completing form SS-4.

## TAXATION

There are various taxation types and benefits depending on your formation type. The most common setup for integrative medicine practitioners is an LLC. Though an LLC helps to protect your personal assets, you may also consider an S corporation tax status to secure tax benefits. LLCs have fewer reporting requirements compared to a corporation. Please note that a single-membered LLC is taxed as a sole proprietorship and self-employed, meaning that income and expenses on personal income are reported and taxes are paid on any profits made by the company. If a single-member LLC is taxed as an S corporation, the single member can be counted as an employee of the business and obtain a salary. Taxes will only be paid on the owner's salary, not all profits, and they will not have taxes on social security or Medicare. S corporation status is an opportunity to save on taxes. As an S corporation, you can take advantage of the "pass-through taxation," wherein profits and losses are part of the owners' personal tax returns. A corporation without S corporation status pays taxes on the entity's income and taxes are paid on income received by the owner or the employee. S corporations are, however, limited to one hundred shareholders, unlike LLCs and corporations.

## MEDICAL MALPRACTICE

After forming your business and receiving your medical license, you can now submit for medical malpractice insurance. It is important to connect with your peers to decide on which medical malpractice companies may be a fit for your particular specialty and location of practice. There are different coverage types for medical malpractice. For example, in the naturopathic medical profession, there are commonly limits of $500,000/$1,500,000 for total incidents up to $1 million by occurrence/$3 million for total incidents. Although medical malpractice companies should be familiar with the details, make sure to check with your Department of Public Health to determine the requirements of medical malpractice for the state you are in.

Medical malpractice will help to protect you from suits against you as a professional for any negligence as it pertains to clinical practice towards a patient. The average cost of medical malpractice varies by specialty area; review your association's guidelines for averages before selecting a company. The cheapest medical malpractice company doesn't necessarily equate to it being the best company to provide your coverage. A few factors to consider include experience with medical professionals and your specialty, a carrier within the state you are practicing, tail coverage, and financial rating. Tail coverage may be a key one, as sometimes the costs are very high if you choose to leave and move to another medical malpractice carrier. Additionally, if you plan to provide services like telemedicine or concierge, you should inquire with your malpractice insurer about their policies toward this and for their coverage in the event an action occurs. Additionally, it is important to look if the medical malpractice covers your full scope of practice that you are trained in, if there are any limitations, or if there are there add-on fees.

## BUSINESS INSURANCES: LIABILITY INSURANCE AND WORKERS COMPENSATION

It is also important to have business liability insurance to protect yourself from lawsuits to the business entity, particularly outside of medical care. This should include coverage for the cost of the lawsuit and the legal expense, and cover at least $1,000,000 of liability. General liability insurance is relatively low for small businesses. General liability insurance covers you for bodily injury (e.g. if someone slips and falls), property damage, damage to premises, medical payments, and sometimes the cost of the operation being affected due to damage to the building or environmental causes, e.g. loss of power for an extended period of time. General liability coverage varies by state location. If you do have employees, you should also have workers compensation, which covers medical expenses and wage loss for an employee that becomes injured or ill due to working with your company. You can often work with the same company for both general liability insurance and workers compensation insurance.

## INSURANCE CREDENTIALING

If you intend to provide insurance in your office, I would suggest beginning the process of filling out the applications by insurance type immediately after receiving your medical license and incorporation, as it may take three months to become empaneled. The first step is to look at completing your information through CAQH; your practitioner information needs to be completed every 120 days. The insurers pull from CAQH to ensure your information is updated and to see if you continue being qualified to carry insurance. The next step would be to contact the credentialing department of each company you hope to get insured with and receive the credentialing application. Make sure a location to provide services is identified prior to completing the application. If the address is changed, it is typically required to complete a form for each insurance company to update the address, and to update accordingly in CAQH. After submitting the application and receiving the contract with your insurance company, carefully read it, particularly the rates per visit. This may be an area in which you would like to negotiate, particularly if you have a group practice with other practitioners. Most insurance agreements have evergreen clauses, but they can be reviewed annually and rene-gotiated at that time.

## INSURANCE VERSUS CASH PAY

There are pros and cons to insurance versus cash-based businesses. The benefit of insurance is that it provides the opportunity for a new practitioner to be able to have their schedule filled in a more expedient manner. However, it also requires a significant administrative burden to submit the bills in a timely fashion to ensure you are paid back for services. Additionally, many insurance companies include high deductibles, meaning you may need to follow up with patients to reimburse you when a deductible has not been met, which could result in a loss of revenue for your business. It is important to have clear operational procedures to handle this and to have the coverage type for each patient, as well as ensuring that you are eligible for reimbursement. Insurance-based companies may increase volume; however, there may be additional costs of having to hire billing support, or having to take up your own time to submit the bills yourself, which is time-consuming as your practice grows. Additionally, it can have a significant impact on the cash flow of the business while waiting for reimbursement or during times in which the service is declined. You may also be limited in providing some additional add-on services, depending on your state and scope, for example, acupuncture or manipulation services. Insurance companies also have the right to audit your charts; if errors are found with coding and billing, they can also request a percentage of past paid bills to be paid back to them. It is always important that codes match the level of service rendered and that your documentation clearly covers this. I have ample experience working with audit requests and reviews, and have learned the importance of regular quality review of charts and documentation.

Cash-based businesses allow more flexibility with adjusting your fees and prices and with the time spent with a patient, as well as a decreased administrative burden. However, that administrative burden may subsequently be placed on marketing, as there will be fewer patient inquiries or individuals that decide to receive care from you when they find that it is not covered by insurance. For this reason, I highly suggest having a specific niche, particularly one that is condition-based, that your practice is known for. This provides the ability for patients seeking support for a specific condition, one that has not been met by seeing other professionals, to see you. But for this to work, you need to speak to their "pain point," and it needs to be unique and have a demonstrated model of effectiveness, where they are willing to pay for the out-of-pocket cost. Many businesses that are successful in this realm often have a slower ramp-up and receive a majority of patients through word-of-mouth and through marketing very intelligently toward their target market. It is also extremely important that your cash-based practice has a proven success record, which is hard to demonstrate when first starting a practice; however, it will build over time, and thus needs to be an area that you absolutely must be committed to, being very strong clinically and an expert in your field.

Some businesses change from insurance-based to cash-based. This is often a tricky process and needs to be carefully planned. Typically, one way is to provide patients with ample advanced notice, around six months. You may also want to decrease the companies you are insured with so as to slowly transition down while working with the insurance companies you prefer. If you have other practitioners in your office, you may not want to have the entire office switch from insurance to a cash-based practice. It may be wiser to have one of the practitioners in the group have insurance so that there is a gradual transition to cash-based. Additionally, you want to ensure that the service that is being offered as cash-based is a worthwhile investment, and that your business is distinguished enough that your patients feel they are willing to forego the use of their insurance company.

*Chapter 4*

# Types of Services

## FEE FOR SERVICE

Fee for service is the most common type of service for business-es. This means that a fee is paid for each service provided; this language applies to both cash-based and insurance-based businesses. For example, thirty minutes, forty-five minutes, etc. by CPT code will be reimbursed. If you are interested in changing the fees and are providing insurance coverage, you would need to reach out directly to the insurance company to negotiate rates. If you have a cash-based business, the rates are typically increased simultaneously for all CPT codes; this should be completed in an organized manner—for example, at the beginning of every year—and in a scheduled way so that patients can expect and prepare for these changes. Some reasons to consider increasing rates are: you have a long wait list (e.g. greater than four to six weeks), your rate has not been updated in many years, it's below the market rate, you serve a very specific niche, etc.

## TELEMEDICINE

Telemedicine is a HIPAA-compliant method to provide care to patients remotely via videoconferencing and telemedicine soft-ware. Telemedicine provides for greater flexibility on both the practitioner's and patient's side, while also providing the same level of high-quality care. Many practitioners either provide a blend of telemedicine services in their clinical practice or use it as the preferred model to deliver care. Each state has different rules as it applies to telemedicine, which may vary by insurance type. Some rules, for example, may require an initial in-person office visit and allow for telemedicine for subsequent visits. If it is clinically necessary to see the patient in-person, it is imperative that you make accommodations to do so. For telemedicine requirements, it is good to look and see if your EMR system has the capability to do so in a secured method and to review your operational procedures to set up. I would suggest looking at both the Department of Public Health standards to provide telemedicine within the state you operate in and your contract with your insurance company. Additionally, make sure to check on your medical malpractice coverage to ensure you are covered in the event of a medically related lawsuit. You may also be required to be licensed in the states that you are seeing via telemedicine, which your malpractice insurer, attorney, and that particular state's regulations can provide guidance on.

## CONCIERGE

Concierge service is both more modern and also a "throwback" to the old ways of how medical care was provided directly in the home. In concierge medicine, there is an annual fee or retainer; these practices are membership specific and cash based. Practitioners manage a panel of patients and are more readily accessible, often 24/7, for the select patients they work with. It is also known as "Fee-for-Care" versus "Fee-for-Service." A patient is typically not able to use a health savings account or flexible spending account like someone can with a "Fee-for-Service" model, even in a cash-based business. Concierge panels may range from as few as twenty-five patients to as many as one thousand. Concierge includes faster access for patients to receive direct care, in-office services, and also for some coordinated care for the emergency room. Ideal candidates for concierge are practitioners in internal medicine or family medicine, but there are plenty of individuals who provide concierge with a distinct specialty. Concierge services are typically for higher-end, affluent clients, which you may want to consider if you plan on serving those along a varied economic spectrum. You are required to carry a license in each state that you provide concierge services to. Additionally, I recommend developing a network of professional resources in all the states you provide concierge to, in the event of an emergency where the patient needs to be seen by someone as soon as possible. You would need to work out a financial arrangement with the practitioner that assists a patient who resides in a state that you are not in close proximity to. Consider if this is of interest to you and a way in which you would like to practice medicine. For me, 24/7 accessibility, even with a low panel, would affect my quality of life, as I like to be able to manage my personal time away from the office. However, I know many practitioners that find that this way of practice provides for a higher level of freedom, flexibility, and quality of life.

## ALTERNATIVE PRACTITIONER SERVICE TYPES

There are varied types of alternative clinical services you may look to provide at your office to augment general integrative medical care. Common clinical services that are helpful to complement your practice include acupuncture, chiropractic, nutrition, Reiki, craniosacral therapy, and physical therapy. Most of these services are physical medicine-oriented and may be difficult for you to incorporate as a practitioner into your regular office visit. Because of this, it's convenient to have these services all together in one place for patients to make use of outside of regular office visits. This provides an opportunity for patients to access a full array of care, meeting all of their needs fully, while also helping to build the growth of your business. It also provides the opportunity for collaboration and lets you refer as necessary between practitioner types. Collaborating across practitioner types in the office requires good boundary setting of which type of service will be provided by what practitioner type. It also takes more effort to manage individual patient care when another practitioner needs to be brought into the discussion, especially if the patient is referred out because a higher level of care is needed or because it's an area of specialty not currently provided at your office.

## ANCILLARY SERVICES

It is helpful to also consider ancillary services that your patients may access independent of your practice. For example, an in-office sauna to help with detoxification, and to allow patients to practice specific protocols with the sauna, intravenous nutrient therapy, laser therapy, far infrared biomats, ozone therapy, PEMF machines, colonic hydrotherapy, etc. may all be services that you wish to establish. These services can often improve the clinical outcomes for patients, and can be managed by a support staff if clear operational procedures have been established. Be mindful of which ancillary services you include and if they meet an immediate need for your patients. I, myself, suffer from shiny object syndrome and have wasted some money on buying great equipment that may not be used for a period of time. Over time, I've learned to specifically seek ancillary services and practitioner services that patients frequently inquire about that seem like a positive adjunct to their care. If you are unable to offer these at your office due to limitations of space or financing, I suggest building a good network to refer patients out to for the services that you feel will improve the clinical outcome for your patients.

## LAB SERVICES

Most integrative medicine practitioners offer specialty lab tests. Commonly seen laboratory tests include stool parasitology testing, hormone testing, salivary cortisol testing, neurotransmitter testing, heavy metal testing, and environmental exposures, such as mold testing; these are good foundational kits to have available in your office. There is also specific bloodwork that may check for nutrients, autoimmune factors, tick-borne infections, and much more that you can offer at your office. If you have limited space, see if you can have kits drop shipped to your patients directly, or carry the lab kits that are most frequently needed at your office. There are multiple options available for providing specialty labs in your office, which should ideally be managed by a staff member, if available.

## MEMBERSHIPS

Some practitioners decide on a membership type model. The membership type model may include regular clinical services or varied service types like acupuncture over the course of the year, or it may include things like discounts on supplements or ancillary services. If you feel that there are products such as this that may be helpful to patients, a membership model for those services may be useful. Memberships of this type are usually looked at monthly, though some are annual. It provides an opportunity for patients to build a greater connection with your practice over a period of time and to support them in meeting their healthcare needs.

## HOLIDAY OFFERINGS

Holidays and special events are opportunities to continue to engage with patients throughout the year. Ensure that you are connecting via email, social media, etc. to help celebrate with your patients. This also leads to an opportunity to provide offers to patients that are relevant and helpful for that specific time of the year. It is also an opportunity to use seasonal workshops and develop a greater sense of community in your practice.

## BUSINESS PRODUCTS: CUPS, SHIRTS, BOOKS, ETC.

Successful integrative practices often offer complimentary products at their offices. Common ones include pens, cups, and shirts. If you have a book that can be provided to patients to assist in their medical care, this is of huge benefit to the patient.

Many doctors self-publish books that can be used as an educational tool for their patients.

## ADVISOR/CONSULTING

There are various opportunities to practice in integrative medicine outside of the clinical setting. Many integrative practitioners may be involved in giving talks about their specific area of focus, or may be asked to be an advisor or liaison for a nutraceutical company based on the patient population they serve. Additionally, doctors may serve as educational consultants for different disease conditions. Consider these opportunities for individuals you frequently partner with, e.g. vendors, based on the population you serve. This is where the importance of building sound networks and connections comes in, as they help to create these opportunities, in addition to regular participation in conferences and your specialty's association.

# Chapter 5

# Marketing and Branding

## DETERMINING LOCATION

When searching for a business location, there are several factors that need to be carefully weighed. Knowing the types of services and products you plan on offering is important, as well as the target market you plan to serve. It's not all about location, location, location. There are several factors to consider; here are some of the most important ones:

- Culture Fit: Does the location match the feel and culture you are looking to offer at your practice? For example, is it laid back, is it family oriented/centered, is it in an office park or a cozy house, or is it about a convenient location and address to provide telemedicine services from or for a home base for a concierge business?

- Target Market: Does the location's demographics match the market you seek to target? For example, if it's a health-focused area, are you located in one that serves that interest? Or if it's a family-based business, is it based in a retirement community or a college town that doesn't match the target market? Is it located next to other healthcare practitioners where you can network and build a referral base? Is it tucked away, or is it in a prominent location? If you have a niche, the prominent location may be less important, versus if you have more of an urgent/acute care center. Is the parking ample for the location or business you are looking to grow? Is it in a residential area where neighbors may be less happy with the foot traffic? Something I personally have had to consider as I've looked at how my business scales is: does it make sense to expand at the current location and does it have the capacity to do so, or does it make more sense to have a different and larger location or satellite office? The process I've used to help make the decision is based on current data, including where my patients are currently living, if we've used the full office capacity, whether we can extend the current hours, if we have feasible parking, and what the five-year-growth expectation is.

- Competitors: It is good to research the area for competitors that provide the same type of services. For example, are there many integrative medicine practitioners within a one-mile radius of where you plan to operate? If so, what is their niche, and is it different than yours? Sometimes having nearby competitors does not matter if the demand is significant enough to warrant the location, or if your niche is very narrowly focused and has little competition for that area.

- Complementary Businesses: Is it in a location where there are many complementary businesses, where you would be able to have individuals walk by and decide on accessing your service? For example, are there health food stores located close by, or other small businesses that you can easily market to?

- Building Questions: If you are looking to rent, it is important to evaluate the overhead costs, which may influence your decision. If you are looking to buy a commercial space, check the ordinances and if there are building repairs that need to be made, that need to be evaluated, or that are expected to be fixed by the time of purchase.

## MARKET ANALYSIS

You should complete a full market and financial analysis before moving to a location and when deciding on offering services for your business. Ultimately, a market analysis improves the chances of success in your business and decreases risk. A market analysis is completed in various ways, including customer segmentation, analysis of purchasing behaviors, and the economic climate and competition. Begin by looking at potential customers and how large the target market is. If the target market size is very small, it may not be a worthwhile location to build a practice unless you feel individuals will travel some distance for your type of service. If it takes greater than thirty minutes to get to your location, are your patients willing to travel the distance, and does it make sense to complete a full market analysis on that location? The following is a list of key steps in conducting a market analysis:

- Check the industry outlook and a national review of your customer segment.

- Identify the target market. Review important demographics like age, income, race, education, shopping patterns, gender, and occupations. Helpful resources include looking at the city's labor statistics, along with the state and local commerce statistics.

- Review your competition. Identify both the advantages and the disadvantages of your business.

- Assess and analyze market data.

  - Pricing

  - Anticipated market share

  - Cash flow

  - Possible focus groups

  - Financial outlook and growth over a one- to three-year timeframe

  - Growth of the industry

It is also important to complete a full SWOT analysis, which stands for strengths, weaknesses, opportunities, and threats. Strengths and weaknesses generally refer to the internal operations of the business, and opportunities and threats refer to the external part of the organization. Key pieces of the SWOT analysis should be reviewed by the following:

- Strengths: What is your niche? How does this niche provide an advantage to you in the market? How do others view your strengths?

- Weaknesses: What would people view as your weaknesses? What are areas for improvement? Are there areas in which your competitors shine that you don't?

- Opportunities: What are the trends in your niche? Are you able to capitalize on these trends? Are there policy changes in your city or state? Are there changes in technology you can take advantage of, or can you get access to services that aren't currently provided?

- Threats: Are there areas in which your competitors outshine you? What are your obstacles, in marketing and financially? Do any of these threats have the ability to close your doors?

Since you have now identified the services you are going to offer, the culture, the mission, and the vision of the organization, you can utilize this helpful information to develop your initial steps of branding and developing a logo for your business. The information obtained from market analysis and SWOT will help influence the branding you choose. The most important part of branding is that it is consistent across all logos, images, and sales and marketing materials, and that it showcases the same message. This includes coverage across all marketing vehicles, like your website and social media presence. I highly suggest working with a brand expert to help brainstorm, identify, and implement your brand identity. Here are some key factors to consider for branding:

- Be specific to your avatar (customer profile) and target consumer, e.g. busy moms, overwhelmed corporate executives, etc.

- Identify your avatar's buying patterns; much of this information can be gathered from the market analysis. Additionally, what are their pain points? What are they not willing to sacrifice or willing to pay for? What are their goals in life, and what inspires and motivates them?

- Develop a brand promise and research other brands within healthcare to gather ideas.

- Create a logo based on the brand. You can work with many highly competent individuals to develop a logo. There are several companies for logo design. Make sure you are clear on your brand, avatar, and brand promise before moving forward with your logo development, or you will spend wasted hours with redesign or a logo that later doesn't match the message you were seeking to convey. It is also helpful for the branding specialist and website person to have a styling guide, which includes a color palette and typography.

- Create a tagline and elevator pitch.

- Ensure that the brand is authentic and reflects your personality.

## WEBSITE

You have now set up all the requisite baseline information to develop a strong website for your business. At this point of the book, you should have already purchased the domain name. The next step is to get a hosting site; there are many hosting options for your website. If you are creating more than one website, I would suggest using the same domain and hosting company. From experience, I've learned it can be quite confusing to manage different domains and hosting sites for multiple URLs. As you develop your website, here are some helpful considerations:

- Make sure your brand message and logo are clearly identifiable on the home page of the website.

- Check that your mission and vision statement are clearly identified on the website.

- Make sure each practitioner's biography is easy to locate on the website. Make sure each practitioner shares their story, experience, passion for medicine, and specialty areas. This is one of the most frequented pages for patients, in addition to testimonials.

- Check that it's clearly navigable. Make sure the page is not slow to load or to toggle between pages. When I first began loading a lot of images to the homepage on my website, the loading time was slow to appear; this is an issue, as most consumers will spend no more than fifteen to thirty seconds on your website, and you want to capture their attention immediately.

- Create landing pages.

- Look at SEO practices for websites and keywords. (I will expand on this below.)

- Ensure that the most important information can be found. Consider which are the most frequently asked questions by patients that should be posted.

- Consider developing landing pages, lead magnets, and opt-ins to build an email list and to engage with potential new patients and existing patients.

- Focus on posting positive patient experiences and testimonials. Patient stories always resonate with the patients you seek to serve because they are often experiencing those very same ailments. Hearing positive stories from other patients prompts the interest of a potential new patient and inspires them to schedule an appointment. I would say this is one of the top benefits of having a website, and it will be the most popular part of your website for patients. I often have patients say they have seen positive patient testimonials on several different sites about our practice before scheduling an appointment. It provides patients with confidence prior to stepping in the door.

## SEARCH ENGINE OPTIMIZATION (SEO)

SEO (Search Engine Optimization) is a strategic area of focus in all parts of business growth and is a worthwhile investment. SEO allows your target market and potential patients to find you easier on search engines, as it lists you higher in search engines. It is important to try to get listed high on the first page, as most consumers do not look past the first handful of listings in a search engine. Working with an SEO expert will help you be identified by keywords that you want your business to be known for. They will also make suggestions on your website design to bring greater traffic to your site. Alternatively, if you have patient testimonials in high-traffic areas that are picked up by popular search engines, or posted on doctor profile sites, this allows you to be listed higher in the SEO ranking without paying for an SEO expert. Be careful when signing up with a SEO specialist, as there are many to choose from. Ask around to see who your peers have used. I have searched long and far and have only recently found a reputable company that has demonstrated their ability to increase my ranking on search engines and the number of requests by patients from finding us online.

*Chapter 6*

# Hiring Staff and Building a Positive Workplace Culture

## STAFFING PLAN

Once you have a strong mission/vision statement and a strategic plan, you can use those to develop a solid staffing plan. A staffing plan is initially an outline of your current staffing arrangement and your projected future growth over the course of one, three, and five years. A staffing plan should ensure that you are able to better meet the operational functions of your business and increase revenue to your business. The plan should also identify specific skillsets needed for positions that you intend to build or hire for. For some, it may mean initially working with virtual assistants, which we will discuss later. Some business owners may not be interested in hiring, based on the model they are hoping to develop. Hiring staff requires an additional administrative burden on you as the owner, and also a skillset of how to inspire, motivate, and retain good hires, and how to terminate as needed. Be sure to carefully and deliberately plan for growth based on your current financials. Also make sure to plan for initial expenses/costs, if you have a grace period to cover those costs, how you will account for costs if there's a greater number of patients that need to be seen, and how this improves the business overall. I've always liked, as part of this process, to create organizational charts that build for growth, so as to have a visual mapping of your staff.

## HIRE A GLORIA: WORKPLACE CULTURE

I've titled this subsection "Hire a Gloria" for a reason: because I believe workplace culture is EVERYTHING, particularly having the right staff to match your mission/vision. The culture should be palpable in your business. For us, it is one of the highest compliments we receive, that they can feel the energy is different in our space, that it feels special, and they feel like they can trust and have confidence in our care. That energy is felt from every part of their interaction with the office, from the initial booking of their new patient appointment with my clinic director, Gloria, to the time they meet the practitioner, to the time they check out, and all the time in between. We let them know that we are a support for them, to not hesitate at all to ask, and that we are equally invested in seeing them well. Patients can feel that, because all staff, including the office staff and doctors, convey that message and also believe it. When you have a good workplace culture, you can see it reflected in your patient testimonials. Make sure your testimonials match the message and mission you are looking to convey.

Some methods by which we've developed a good workplace culture include having regular morning huddles with affirmations/quotes for the day, scheduling team outings and lunches, ensuring the team feels respected, establishing a collaborative work culture, and proceeding with the intention and goal of ensuring they are happy with their work and have the opportunity to grow and learn. I've had over a decade of experience working as a healthcare executive, and at one point had over eighty staff under my purview. I have extensive experience hiring, retaining, and also letting go of employees. Some of the key values I've implemented as an administrator, and have felt with staff that have worked with me, are trust, integrity, ethics, fairness, and appreciation. These are things I'm fully committed to, and they have a trickledown effect. Remember, leadership starts from the top, so if staff are not showcasing the culture you want patients to feel, consider what you are doing to help mentor them through implementing your culture, creating performance plans, or walking your talk. Ultimately, everything comes back to you, and a positive mindset and commitment to the mission/vision is felt more by what is shown than by what is said.

## EMPLOYEES

After you determine the staffing plan, it is time to hire more employees, and to further develop current ones if you already have staff. Employees that you should initially hire should include staff to answer phones and book appointments; additional staff may be needed if you plan on having another doctor or nurse practitioner for your office. Generally, the minimum should be one half-time staff member for every two practitioners. Also, depending on the extent of services, you may need clinical support staff to help with areas like checking vitals, working as a scribe, or overseeing alternative therapies if those are offered, like IV nutrients. Ensure that the cost of these positions will be lower than the expected revenue these services will provide, as with IV nutrients, or that they make the workload simpler for the practitioners. It is also important to ascertain with these additional offerings what bandwidth your team has to accommodate these services, and/or if it will lower efficiencies in other parts of the operations of your business. It is also helpful to hire support staff that may have several competencies, e.g. a medical assistant that can answer phones, book appointments, and support some clinical functions. Each state has different rules when it comes to use of clinical support, so ensure that you check with state regulations. With employees, there are several factors you will need to consider, including if it's part-time or full-time employment, if benefits will be provided, a probation timeframe, performance evaluations, employee manuals, and workers compensation, amongst other factors.

## VIRTUAL ASSISTANTS (VAS)

Virtual assistants (VAs) are a useful initial step when starting your business, and also with growing your business. There are multiple options when working with a virtual assistant, including a retainer and hourly roles. A virtual assistant can be used for various types of responsibilities, including answering the phones, booking appointments, accepting insurance, handling sales and marketing, doing market research, managing your calendar, responding to emails, and so forth. In my experience, I have always preferred a retainer with a specified amount per month, so it is easier to manage expenses. I also put together a template for every function; for example, a template on how to answer phones and schedule appointments, as well as frequently asked questions for them to refer to when on the phone. I would also suggest that monthly, at a minimum, ideally weekly, you connect to see what questions have come up or how processes can be improved. You want to ensure that your virtual assistant is efficient and prompt and can represent the brand the same way a staff person in-office would be able to. Some things that can help with this is to set up an initial one to two hour meeting during which you provide the script of how you want them to answer the phone and review it, in addition to roleplaying a conversation. Additionally, properly screen the virtual assistants you are looking to work with. For example, were they recommended by others? If they were not, ask for a list of references. Inquire what they expect cost wise, based on business volume and potential growth, and also get a good idea of how they sound on the phone and if their culture matches the culture you have created or are looking to create. There are various virtual assistant companies and independent virtual assistants I have worked with; it requires a lot of upfront time to be most effective, as the individual is not with you every day, so they can know all of the ins and outs and also adopt all of the practices of your office. You need to be willing to invest this time to have a successful partnership with a VA, and additionally know when the right time is to discontinue services if it is not meeting your needs.

## CONTRACTORS

I absolutely love contractors. Contractors have allowed me to maintain my business and provide expert knowledge. I generally suggest working with individuals who are referred to you from other practitioners. I also suggest that for each contractor type, you review at least two different contractors to compare their services and scope. Additionally, though they are not employees, I try as much as possible to ensure that the contractors I work with fit well into the culture of my business. An effective contractor can essentially feel like a key member of the team. You may need to work with contractors that have a deep level of specialty you can't get elsewhere; for example, I have a health-care law firm that is able to guide me in areas like compliance, medical services, and licenses.

These are some suggestions for your initial hiring of contractors:

- Bookkeeping services: A bookkeeper helps to pay bills, manage your books, e.g. Quickbooks, produce financial statements for your review, and, depending on their level of expertise, may submit quarterly reports of sales and use tax reports. They should have the ability to work closely with an accountant. If you can't afford an accountant initially, the bookkeeper would be the first initial step, but you will need an accountant to at least submit your annual taxes.

- Accountant: An accountant will carefully review financial statements, make recommendations on expenses and costs that may be cut, and file taxes, including quarterly reports and annual taxes. They will analyze data, help with decisions on financing for new expenses, e.g. new hires or buying commercial property/building, and help facilitate any audits. I have found both my accountant and bookkeeper to be some of the most key individuals I work with, and they fully represent the culture of the business. It is important that the contractors you are working with are ones that you trust, who have integrity and are invested in your business. It is also important to regularly check your financials and to not remove yourself fully from evaluating on a regular daily and weekly basis.

- Lawyers: I have numerous lawyers, and suggest that any business owners and practitioners do, too. Particularly in healthcare, you may need a contract / transactional lawyer; a healthcare specific lawyer to answer questions related to HIPAA compliance, healthcare contracts, licenses, and malpractice questions in conjunction with your carrier; a real estate attorney (if you're making a commercial purchase); and a general attorney you can regularly communicate with, if needed. This is not something you want to skimp on, as it can have a significant negative impact on your business. You do not want to solely rely on legal advice from your peers, social media posts, or Google searches; there are many intricacies that can only be fully understood by an attorney that knows your business well.

- Human resources (HR) consultant: As you hire employees, it is helpful to hire an HR consultant to help manage workplace issues. HR consultants can help with various areas like hiring and onboarding new employees, making performance evaluations, developing an employee handbook, handling salary and benefit compensation, providing guidance for employees, and arranging disciplinary action and termination procedures. They can also help you build a staffing plan, advise, and recommend when an HR attorney may be needed. Furthermore, they can help to identify and develop your workplace culture and provide various trainings like sexual harassment seminars. It is important to contract with an HR expert sooner rather than later; you do not want to have to seek an HR consultant after an issue arrives, such as termination of an employee. An HR consultant in particular is someone you want to fully know the culture of your business and what current HR practices are in place, and to guide appropriately. Many make the mistake of seeking an HR consultant only when there is an issue, much like with a lawyer, rather than establishing a relationship beforehand. Additionally, some workplace or personnel issues could have been managed or prevented if an HR consultant was contracted earlier in the process.

- Business development consultant: I have found it quite helpful to have a business development consultant as I grew my business. They provide an objective lens and analyze your current target market, whether services are meeting demand, what areas are growing in the market, and what opportunities you should capitalize on. They can also analyze financial numbers as it pertains to deciding on staff hires, particularly doctors, and determine which is the greatest opportunity to focus on.

- Website designer: A website designer is usually brought in earlier in the process, after some of the other key factors of the business have been identified. It is helpful for the website designer to have your branding information, style guide, and overall feel of the message you are trying to convey on your website. There are many companies that help to develop websites, increase SEO, help with patient surveys/testimonials, and build things like lead magnets and opt-ins. As with the VAs, it's important to initially spend time with them for them to have a greater understanding of your business.

- Information Technology (IT): As your business grows, it is important to look at IT personnel that can ensure your system is secured, particularly as it pertains to HIPAA information, establish and backup your computers, and keep all IT systems updated regularly. They may also provide advice on trends that can make processes with your business more efficient. IT consultants can work hourly or on a retainer based. I typically hire a consultant as a retainer for a number of hours, and increase those hours if we know additional staff are onboarding or if there's a need to update the systems.

- Marketing and sales consultant: A marketing consultant may help with branding, social media, email campaigns, the design of your website, business cards, flyers, and other materials that showcase your brand message. A marketing consultant can be a key person for your business growth and will also be important to develop an ongoing relationship with. Some businesses choose to hire a part-time sales position or consultant for sales to acquire new leads. This may be helpful to build networks and contacts, and to engage new potential clients.

# Chapter 7

# Operations and Finance

## STARTUP COSTS AND FINANCING

There are basic startup costs that need to be considered when beginning your business, as well as the financing needed to do so. There are multiple ways to accumulate capital. Oftentimes, personal financing and savings are needed to initially cover the basic costs to deliver care to patients. Examples of sources of funding include crowdfunding, angel investor networks, bank lending, grants, and venture capital. It is often difficult to get a sizeable amount through bank lending for an initial startup business; however, a solid business plan may provide the opportunity to have a greater level of funding provided. It is helpful to work with a bank that you already have an established account with since you will have a long-term relationship with them. Please make sure to carefully review the interest rates and payback time, and if you think your financial projections can cover the cost back to the bank. You may also want to look at credit lines of services from a personal credit card at a zero percent APR or small APR rate for a year, which may be more feasible than a bank; however, be mindful again of paying it back, or your credit could be damaged or you could become bankrupt if you're unable to pay.

Informal sources of financing include personal finances (i.e. bootstrapping), family and friends, and crowdfunding. If you are using your personal financing, be sure to plan, save, and estimate anticipated costs before you operationalize your business. Personal financing provides for accountability to self and flexibility in spending. With a more formal capital financing, there is a financial responsibility by the organization who lends to invest in credible sources; these include grants, angel investors, credit unions, banks, and traditional lenders. Carefully project the costs you need to start your business, both in the initial startup and over the course of the year. Here is a list of example startup costs for a medical office:

- EMR system
- Furniture to fit office
- Medical equipment
- Technology
- Website design
- Office rent and utilities, plus a security deposit if renting
- Phones
- Supplements for a dispensary
- Laboratory supplies
- Improvements or renovations to existing medical practice
- Sales and marketing: business cards, flyers

- Initial legal expense
- Insurance and business taxes
- General operational expenses

## SETTING UP MEDICAL PRACTICE AND PATIENT FLOW

In addition to startup costs to begin your business and a general office setup, there are some other important operational practices that should be established. For example, it is important to identify clear operational procedures, create an appointment scheduling process, and manage patient flow. Identifying key front desk processes and activities will particularly help when you're hiring a new staff by making your expectations clear, and will allow staff to optimize their effectiveness in their position. For example, for front desk staff it is important to provide a call and booking script to identify how patients should be scheduled, e.g. leaving time for new patients, established patients, acute visits, etc., and how to handle booking. It is critical to establish the process, from scheduling, to when the doctor sees the patient, to the checkout process, as well as the follow-up. If you choose to cover insurance, identify the process for billing, the collection of all information from patients for the insurance payment, etc.

Here are some key first steps:

- New patient intake form, both adult and pediatric; or, you may also have different intake forms sorted by type of condition.

- HIPAA and notice of privacy practices
- Informed consent
- Medical records release
- EMR system: set up basic templates
- A method for communication with patients, e.g. portals
- Business cards and appointment reminders for checkout
- Patient handouts and instructions
- Visual frameworks to utilize during patient visits
- Superbill with CPT and ICD codes
- Letterhead and envelopes
- Form or email for patient survey/testimonial regarding their experience

## POLICIES AND PROCEDURES

It is important to set up baseline policies and procedures for your business. Policies and procedures help to have clear rules that staff can follow and creates accountability. The procedures should at least include sales, operations, technology, and HR policies. These are considered standard operating procedures (SOPs) or policies and procedures (P & Ps). It is helpful to build general, core SOPs and add to them monthly so it is less overwhelming and time consuming. SOPs should be reviewed at least annually and be approved in conjunction with the Board if you are operating an S corporation or regular corporation.

Here are some key examples of policies and procedures for medical practices:

- Business strategic goal and mission statement
- Documentation format and requirements
- Patient rights and responsibilities
- Appointment system
- Safety procedures
- Ethical boundaries, including sexual harassment
- Discrimination policies
- Privacy and confidentiality
- Medical records release
- Instructions for handling patient discharge
- Physical plant and equipment
- Quality improvement and review of records
- Human resources policies
- EMR policies

## EMR SYSTEMS AND PORTALS

You should evaluate multiple electronic medical record (EMR) systems and assess if they fit with your clinical questioning, assessment, and operational flow. If you are completing labs for patients, check if it has a lab interface and faxing ability; or if you are writing prescriptions, determine if it has the ability to send them electronically. Additionally, several of the EMR systems for integrative doctors are not set up to meet the medical records charting requirements. Make sure to have the mandated requirements available, and then consider other factors like your ease of ability to navigate it, its visual appearance, and its ability to correspond and interact with patients via a portal. You may also want to ensure that it can run reports to gather helpful information about patients, like how many new patients booked in a month or what were some commonly seen conditions, or for meeting federal requirements for your business.

## HUMAN RESOURCES (HR) POLICIES AND PROCEDURES

Basic human resource (HR) policies and procedures should be created even at the onset of a new business with no employees. Initial HR policies include sexual harassment, non-discrimination, and equality standards. When hiring staff, HR policies related to hiring, pay, discipline, grievance, termination, drugs and alcohol, non-disclosure agreements, whistleblowing, sick and vacation time, training and development, bullying, and use of company facilities, amongst others, should be considered.

*Chapter 8*

# Compliance

## LEGAL REQUIREMENTS FOR A MEDICAL PRACTICE

It is helpful to consider compliance-related policies related to ethics, HIPAA, anti-kickback, and other required reporting. Make sure your license continues to be active, the educational requirements for your license are upheld, and that your facility licenses are maintained and managed as well. For compliance policies, it is important to maintain patient rights and privacy and to prevent fraud and abuse by submitting claims regarding services that do not match with what was rendered. Compliance also entails review of contracts and legal agreements, particularly in partnership relationships with another organization or when working with contractors/consultants. It also includes management of lease agreements and debt agreements owed. If you run a fully operating lab, make sure to review CLIA and other safety requirements. Attorneys that have a compliance-specific focus may also assist with the process for the discharging of patients and subpoenas. Make sure you are knowledgeable of anti-kickback statutes and compliance with the Stark law as well.

## HEALTH INSURANCE PROFITABILITY AND ACCOUNTABILITY ACT

The Health Insurance Portability and Accountability Act (HIPAA) is an important set of practices to uphold within your organization that ensures the integrity of your business. HIPAA includes privacy and confidentiality, policies, keeping of records, and safety within IT systems. It is important to post privacy practices, and all patients must sign a Notice of Privacy Practices in order for you to provide care, as well as coordinate care that is clinically emergent. HIPAA includes a set of standards and requirements with clear statutory and regulatory rules. You should also familiarize yourself with 42 CFR, which speaks to the higher level of confidentiality and documentation for specific areas related to substance abuse. There are also unique guidelines for adolescents and confidentiality when receiving healthcare for sensitive topics such as pelvic examinations, STIs, and substance use. Parents will potentially have access to these documents upon request if the adolescent is under the age of eighteen and using insurance, since they will be under the parents' policy. You can review the medical record in advance of providing a copy. Make sure to review the guidelines specific to the state in which you practice.

Please be mindful of the documentation you are required to provide; as a note, always provide what is minimally necessary. Documentation for employment should be succinct, and a form for the request should be sent in addition to the patient release. This same consideration applies to subpoenas and court appearances; there are minimal notice requirements and timeframes that can be discussed in conjunction with your attorney.

Subpoenas also require a medical records release and consent from the patient.

## PREPARING FOR MEDICAL RECORDS REQUESTS AND AUDITS

Having policies and procedures regarding documentation standards will help you to adhere to good quality standards for medical records. Regular qualitative checks should be completed for medical records to confirm that the coding is consistent with the complexity and services rendered. If you do provide insurance coverage, a representative from an insurance company may ask for a copy of a medical record to audit and assess, or may appear on site. Remember that they still need to follow the requirements for HIPAA and should only be permitted access to or a copy of the specific medical record they are looking to review. Also ensure that documents are provided from the reviewer/auditor to confirm that you are permitted to furnish this information.

## ETHICS

As a practitioner and as someone running a medical practice, good ethics and integrity are important standards to uphold. Make sure to look at your specialty association's rules and guidelines on this. There are some basic principles of medical ethics, including that you provide the patient with a fully informed decision of all the risks and benefits of procedures, that what you do does not harm the patient, that you have good intentions with the patients you serve, and that fairness is upheld, including treating any research subjects equally; these are based on the four major principles for ethics for medical professionals. Ethics is based on the core foundation as practitioners that we are maintaining professional excellence and integrity, and are not working in only our best personal or financial interests when it pertains to providing the right clinical care for the patients we serve.

## CONTRACTS

When running an integrative medical practice, you will have multiple contract types that you manage. Some contracts will include insurance company contracts (if you are providing insurance), leasing contracts, contracts for independent contractors, and, potentially, memorandums of understanding (MOUs). Contracts always provide an opportunity to negotiate and to add additional content that was previously not identified or that has changed since initiating the contract. Contracts should be carefully reviewed by yourself and your attorneys. Practitioners also may look into setting up business associate agreements (BAA) with companies who access information needed to evaluate their business. If you are working with contractors, you should ensure that privacy and nondisclosure agreements are in place. If they have not been set up previously, ensure that you establish the right standards and agreements going forward.

*Chapter 9*

# Supplement Dispensaries

## CHOOSING TO HAVE A SUPPLEMENT DISPENSARY: PROS AND CONS

There are numerous benefits to having a dispensary for supplements, which includes nutritional supplements, herbal therapies, and homeopathy, amongst others. The most important is that building a dispensary for an integrative medical practice allows patients to receive a high-quality product that has been third party tested, unlike many other supplements on the market. On the other hand, you need to carefully manage the cost of providing supplements to patients; even if it is online, there is still an administrative burden. Many integrative practitioners provide a blend of in-office supplements and an online dispensary for patients to utilize for their practice.

## SETTING UP AN IN-OFFICE SUPPLEMENT DISPENSARY

In-office dispensaries are becoming less popular, as online dispensaries provide more convenience and less potential overhead costs. It is often helpful for patients to be able to pick up supplements at the office, but managing inventory and ensuring enough is in stock requires careful management; for this setup, it is ideal if you have an office with ample front desk support.

An in-office dispensary can also cause inconsistent cash flow issues, since supply and demand can change month-to-month. It does allow for continued engagement and relationship building with patients and better management of their care. Patients often appreciate this as an additional benefit, since they are able to check out with their products in hand, and it does provide convenience if you are a locally based business wherein patients can pick up supplements easily from the office.

It is important to have a carefully managed tracking system with your in-office dispensary. This should include measures like scanners to track inventory, reports on par values, daily and weekly reconciliation, and a physical, manual monthly check of products in inventory. It can be a tedious process, but your supplement dispensary needs to be carefully managed to ensure you are covering the cost of providing it in-office.

When your practice offers a fully in-office supplement dispensary, patients need to be mindful of when they are running out of supplements, which can affect continuity of care if lapsed. Patients may often buy low-quality products elsewhere, with different constituents, and you want to ensure that the source they are accessing their supplement from is a credible, high-quality brand, even if they pick it up elsewhere.

In-office dispensaries also require careful management when it comes to mailing items from the office in an expedient manner. It is important that all items, particularly refrigerated ones, are mailed and delivered within a two-to-three-day timeframe; this may require an additional administrative burden that your team will need to manage. The best process is to select specific times of the day that these packages are picked up or delivered and inform patients of the mailing process to facilitate this process smoothly.

## SETTING UP AN ONLINE SUPPLEMENT DISPENSARY

An online dispensary is the wave of the future. Patients and consumers are used to purchasing items online and receiving them in a short period of time. It lowers the administrative burden of having the products in-office and reduces the cost. It is important, though, to continue to look at how you are managing patients within those visits, and that they are still having positive health outcomes, the same as if they were presenting in the office itself. Though this enables some convenience, it also places a higher burden of responsibility on the patient to manage ordering supplements on their own. There is also a generational gap and usability factor with online orders which need to be taken into consideration, based on the population you plan to serve.

## BUILDING A SUPPLEMENT DISPENSARY LIST

When considering the dispensary list for an in-office inventory, consider foundational items and supplements that are frequently recommended. For example, if you commonly see patients for women's health, make sure you maintain at least a minimal stock of commonly recommended herbs in-office for the protocols you recommend. Here is a list of foundational supplements that may be helpful to have on-site:

1. Multivitamins and minerals

2. Probiotics

3. B Complexes

4. Adaptogens

5. GI support supplements

6. Herbs and homeopathy as acute remedies to provide when a patient presents with a more immediate issue.

7. Tinctures: five to ten core botanical extracts

## PRIVATE/WHITE LABEL

In addition to online dispensaries, many practitioners have begun providing more products via private label. Private label allows you to brand your company specifically, which allows for consistency and for you to offer custom-made formulations for your patients. There are many options/vendors to use for private label; however, many require a minimum order level, and you will have to plan in advance for when you feel your inventory stores may be lower. This requires careful management of inventory cost, much like with an in-office dispensary, but has a higher level of complexity.

# Chapter 10

# Scaling Your Business: One-, Three-, and Ten-Year Goalsetting

When you initially begin your business development, it is focused on the mission/vision and strategy, tailored primarily for the first year. As your business grows, though, it is highly important to build out a plan over time: a one-year, three-year, five-year, and ten-year plan. A helpful way to navigate this is by setting specific goals that are reviewed weekly and looking at the full strategic plan once a year. Review of a plan over time will help for you to decide on hiring decisions and other growth opportunities. Your goals may vary from year to year, and it is important to not lose sight of this as your business begins to scale and ramp up. Another helpful tip is to create a milestone checklist for every year with the big-picture ideas that you are looking to grow into or develop over time.

I usually suggest for practitioners to draft a visual schematic of their long-term dream goals and immediate one-year goals; this visual schematic helps to shed light on what the core areas of immediate focus are and how they build into the long-term end goal. Your visual schematic should be inclusive of not only your business goals, but also your personal goals. The plan should also include what you envision for your life, such as your dreams and goals, your empire, and the legacy you plan to leave behind.

# Thank You

This book was inspired by you, integrative medicine practitioners who seek to fully improve others' health, listen to patient needs, and change the current healthcare landscape. Thank you; I appreciate you and I wish you nothing but success in sharing your passion with the world.

# About the Author

Dr. Jaquel Patterson is a nationally and internationally renowned naturopathic physician, coach, and sought-after speaker. She owns a successful multidisciplinary medical practice and has over a decade of experience as a healthcare executive in operations, compliance, integrated care, and quality improvement, and continues to be active in healthcare policy in the state. Dr. Jaquel is the current president of the American Association of Naturopathic Physicians and has been on the boards of several medical associations. She combines her expertise in business and medicine in both her practice and when she is coaching and mentoring others.

Dr. Jaquel received her undergraduate degree from Cornell University in applied economics and management, MBA from Quinnipiac University, doctorate degree in naturopathic medicine from the University of Bridgeport, and her certificate in women's entrepreneurship from Cornell University. In her free time, she enjoys photography, traveling, exercising, and spending time with her family.

Learn more at www.drjaquelnd.com

9 781644 841921

## CREATING DISTINCTIVE BOOKS
## WITH INTENTIONAL RESULTS

We're a collaborative group of creative masterminds
with a mission to produce high-quality books to position
you for monumental success in the marketplace.

Our professional team of writers, editors, designers,
and marketing strategists work closely together to ensure
that every detail of your book is a clear representation
of the message in your writing.

### Want to know more?
Write to us at info@publishyourgift.com
or call (888) 949-6228

Discover great books, exclusive offers, and more at
**www.PublishYourGift.com**

Connect with us on social media

@publishyourgift